UNTOLD STORIES,

CID

LOS ANGELES

UNTOLD STORIES,
CID
LOS ANGELES

THE IRS NOBODY KNOWS TOLD BY SOMEONE WHO DOES KNOW

AL RUSSO

UNTOLD STORIES, CID LOS ANGELES
THE IRS NOBODY KNOWS TOLD BY SOMEONE WHO DOES KNOW

iUniverse books may be ordered through booksellers or by contacting:

iUniverse
1663 Liberty Drive
Bloomington, IN 47403
www.iuniverse.com
844-349-9409

Because of the dynamic nature of the Internet, any web addresses or links contained in this book may have changed since publication and may no longer be valid. The views expressed in this work are solely those of the author and do not necessarily reflect the views of the publisher, and the publisher hereby disclaims any responsibility for them.

Any people depicted in stock imagery provided by Getty Images are models, and such images are being used for illustrative purposes only.
Certain stock imagery © Getty Images.

ISBN: 978-1-6632-6024-6 (sc)
ISBN: 978-1-6632-6025-3 (e)

Library of Congress Control Number: 2024902887

Print information available on the last page.

iUniverse rev. date: 03/06/2024

CONTENTS

ACKNOWLEDGEMENTS

This book would not have been possible without the help and contributions of many, many people. I want to specifically thank the following people, for without their help I'd still be floundering in the book writing process:

1. Pete Tagni
2. Robert J. Perry
3. Jack Devine
4. James Bamford
5. Michael & Sheila Sobel
6. Alan Lipkin
7. Adam Dawson
8. John Everett
9. Bruce Kelton
10. JP
11. Jerry Petievich
12. Marty Laffer

DEDICATION

This book is dedicated to the men and women of the law enforcement arm of the Internal Revenue Service, both past and present.

Dennis Dixon is referenced in this book. He is described as being one of the best and the brightest. Dennis passed away in mid-2023. He, along with former Assistant United States Attorney Bob Perry, put the Los Angeles office of the IRS, Criminal Investigation Division on the map by pioneering the use of "Follow-the-money" techniques in investigating major narcotics traffickers and their money laundering associates. With the unfaltering support of the Chief, Branch Chiefs and Group Managers, the Los Angeles office led the way regarding these types of investigations and caused other CID offices around the country to follow suit. This book is specifically dedicated to Dennis for his investigative ingenuity and leadership in the investigations of major narcotics traffickers and associated money laundering organizations.

This book is also dedicated to my family and particularly to my wife who endured countless hours of me hold up in my office writing this book.

INTRODUCTION

The law enforcement arm of the Internal Revenue Service has been known by several different names over the years. At its inception in 1919 it was called the Special Intelligence Unit of the Bureau of Internal Revenue. The first agents assigned to this unit were former Postal Inspectors. In fact, the very first Chief of the Special Intelligence Unit was Elmer L. Irey, a former Postal Inspector. As the years went by, this unit of the Internal Revenue Service took on various names, including the Internal Revenue Service, Intelligence Division; the Internal Revenue Service, Criminal Investigations Division; and the Internal Revenue Service, Criminal Investigations, its current name. For the purposes of this book, the law enforcement arm of the Internal Revenue Service will be referred to as Criminal Investigation Division, or CID.

No matter its name, this element of the Internal Revenue Service has always had the distinction of having the best financial investigators in all the world. Its number one mission has always been to investigate allegations of criminal violations of the internal revenue laws. Over the years, it has had other tasks assigned to it, such as investigating violations of the money laundering laws and Bank Secrecy Act laws. At various times also it has enforced laws pertaining to the wagering excise tax.

Becoming a Special Agent with the Internal Revenue Service is not an easy task. It goes without saying that a candidate for the position of Special Agent must be physically fit. A candidate must have at least a bachelor's degree. The major subject area is not necessarily important. What is important and required is that the candidate has successfully completed at least 15 semester units of college level accounting. In addition, the candidate must have completed at least an additional 9 semester units of related business courses. And, the candidate must have a college level GPA of at least 2.8. There are also age requirements. The candidate must be at least 21 years old at the time the candidate completes the training academy. The candidate cannot be older than 37 years old. The 37 years old age limit goes to the mandatory retirement age of 57 years old and the retiree must have at least 20 years of service as a Special Agent to qualify for federal law enforcement retirement benefits. The candidate must pass a background and criminal history check, as well as a pre-employment medical exam and a pre-employment drug test. Further, each candidate must pass a pre-employment tax examination and must be legally allowed to carry a firearm.

Candidates for the position of Special Agent with IRS-CI, if the above referenced requirements are met, are then subjected to at least one pre-employment interview. The interview(s) are conducted by a panel of senior managers of IRS-CI. If the candidate successfully completes all of the above referenced requirements and passes the background investigation, the candidate is qualified to be hired as a Special Agent.

Newly minted Special Agents currently attend Special Agent Basic Training at the National Criminal Investigation Training

Academy, located in Glynco, Georgia. The author attended his initial training in Washington, DC during the Watergate era. The training modules consist of pre-basic training, criminal investigator training, and special agent investigative techniques. The entire initial training process can take up to about six months to complete. The final phase of training, special agent investigative techniques, is about 14 weeks long.

Although this book reflects the activities of one former Special Agent, virtually all Special Agents of the criminal arm of the Internal Revenue Service may have had similar experiences and were assigned to similar type cases. This book specifically details cases involving the author, but this type of case work was not and currently is not unique to him.

The criminal investigation arm of the IRS has been involved in many, many notable cases over the years. Some of the more higher profile cases generated lots of publicity. The Al Capone case is probably the most famous criminal case in the history of the IRS. Other notable criminal cases involved Chuck Berry, a very famous entertainer; Joseph Nunan, a former IRS Commissioner; Spiro Agnew, a former vice-president of the United States; and Daryl Strawberry, a former high-profile major league baseball player. More currently, the son of a sitting President of the United States was investigated by IRS-CI. However, there are countless other criminal cases of note that did not receive much, if any, publicity. A few of these matters are discussed in this book, The Untold Stories of CID, Los Angeles.

The Untold Stories of CID, Los Angeles is divided into two sections, reflecting two program areas in which enforcement activity took place. The two sections reflected in this book are Strike Force and Narcotics Money Laundering. There are other program areas of enforcement in which CID has been involved, such as right-wing extremists (tax protestors), terrorist financing, corrupt politicians, and more.

SECTION ONE

STRIKE FORCE

THE LONDON FOG
THAT GOT AWAY

In the mid- to late-1970s, as a Los Angeles based IRS-CID Special Agent, I spent more than a year in a quasi-undercover capacity in an attempt to gather information pertaining to the Los Angeles Mafia Family. As a Sicilian, I could speak and understand enough of the Sicilian dialect to pass scrutiny. I never actually attempted to infiltrate the Family. As a federal law enforcement officer living in Los Angeles, my cover would have been blown very quickly because I was a known commodity in law enforcement circles and also known by bad guys.

I coached youth football in my spare time. One example of the likelihood of my real identity being compromised if I tried to infiltrate the L.A. mob involved an assistant coach on one of my youth football teams. I didn't know it at the time that he volunteered to coach with me, but I later learned that he was a close associate of a well-known Los Angeles based mafia associate. Together they operated a large-scale loan sharking business, as well as organizing bookmakers who paid tribute to these two guys in order to continue their bookmaking activities. This assistant coach had two sons on my team and he in fact attempted to persuade me to allow another mafia associate to help coach the team. I said no.

Another example of my vulnerability to my identity being compromised pertained to an incident when Vinny, a bartender at Cy's Rubio Lounge where I spent a great deal of time, wanted to register his son to play youth football. Vinny approached me when I was helping to sign up football players. He brought his son to the signups and immediately recognized me as a guy who hung out at Cy's. He was cordial and we talked about the youth football program. His son was too big and too old to qualify to play on one of our teams.

However, I still was well positioned to gather intelligence and was tasked to hang out at bars where members of the Los Angeles Mafia family and their friends gathered. But I was always on the outside looking in. I did gather some interesting intelligence that was passed on to the Los Angeles Organized Crime Strike Force. The information included associations that I observed based on who met with whom at Cy's Rubio Lounge.

Most of my undercover activities centered around Cy's Rubio Lounge. Cy's was located in the back of a strip mall on Ventura Boulevard in Encino, California. The mall sat at the corner of Ventura Boulevard and Rubio Street, with a Tony Roma's restaurant out front. There was a fairly large parking lot at the rear of this strip mall, directly behind Cy's Rubio Lounge. Cy's was a typical looking bar, with a long bar and bar stools located on the left as you entered. Directly above the bar was the typical bar glasses holder, containing all different types of glasses that were used in the drink making process. Behind the bar was an extremely large display of bottles of liquor. Every conceivable type of single malt and blended scotch whiskey, bourbon, gin, vodka, and the like were available at Cy's. There was a mirror behind the shelving where the bottles of liquor were kept. This made it appear that there was a larger inventory of liquor bottles than actually displayed. And, there were several refrigerators located below the liquor bottles display that held bottled and canned beer, white wine, and other beverages needing refrigeration.

There were several tables with multiple chairs at each that were placed immediately ahead of the entrance. Beyond the tables and towards the back of the bar was a hallway. The restrooms and an office were directly off of the hallway. At the end of the hallway was another door leading to Rubio Street. This door was seldom used, but it provided a handy escape route if someone had to leave Cy's quickly without using the main entrance.

I hung out at Cy's several times a week. I wasn't there every day, but I was there at least 3 or 4 times each week. I usually would arrive at Cy's between 3 and 4 p.m. and then leave after all of the subjects of interest had departed unless something of interest was happening, in which case I would stay longer. I never carried my weapon while in Cy's. I just didn't need it and I felt somewhat secure in that I seemed to fit right in. But, I never forgot who I was and who the folks that hung out at Cy's were. So, I was always alert to any potential danger. I think that I passed the "Smell test" with my Sicilian banter back and forth with Vinny the bartender. And, for all those at Cy's who "Knew" me, I was an accountant so having a weapon would have been unusual if the bulge in the right back side of my jacket was seen. Also, the slits in the rear section of the sports coats or suit jackets that I wore would have more likely than not exposed the weapon lodged in the right rear section of my trousers. And, I've had unfortunate accidents where my weapon would simply fall out of my trousers on to the floor. The folks that I was interested in at Cy's were very observant, always trying to identify who the cops were. It would only have been a matter of time before someone at Cy's would have noticed that I had a weapon beneath my jacket.

Cy's was the hangout of Michael Rizzitello (Mike Rizzi), Tommy Ricciardi (TR), and occasionally Jimmy Fratianno (Jimmy The Weasel), along with other organized crime figures and wannabes. At the time, Mike Rizzi was reputed to be the head of the Los Angeles Mafia Family; at least that was the assessment of most of the law enforcement community that followed organized crime activities in the Los Angeles area. The Los Angeles Police Department's Organized Crime Intelligence Division (OCID) was convinced that Mike Rizzi was the boss. There were some law enforcement folks who thought that Peter John Milano headed up the L.A. Family, but most thought the boss was Mike Rizzi.

Tommy Ricciardi was a stone-cold killer for the mob. Jimmy Fratianno was alleged to be a major west coast Mafia figure who was based in the San Francisco Bay Area but came to Los Angeles from time to time to hang out at Cy's with his fellow mobsters. Also hanging out at Cy's was one Bobby C. He was a wannabe who wanted to be accepted by Rizzi, Ricciardi and the other Mafia folks. And of course, there were hordes of other wannabes. These were people who wanted to hang out with the real mob guys and assist them with the hope of someday being accepted by them.

One Friday evening when I was at Cy's, Tommy Ricciardi walked into a very crowded gathering of Cy's clientele. "Regular" folks would have drinks at Cy's after work during happy hour probably with the hope of spotting some of the Mafia guys. The crowd parted to let Ricciardi walk through. Virtually everyone in Cy's knew who Tommy was. He was a handsome man, who could have passed as Robert Mitchum's twin brother.

Tommy stopped directly behind where I was standing and in conversation with another patron. I could hear Tommy making small talk with others standing nearby. The small talk included "How's your family?" "Who did you like at Santa Anita today?" "How's business?"

A barmaid approached Tommy and asked him if he wanted a drink. Tommy asked for a Dewar's and water. The barmaid disappeared, supposedly to get Tommy's drink. Tommy continued to talk with people who came over to say hello. Everyone wanted to say hi to Tommy, with the exception of a few people who were afraid to be in his presence. Those who did stop to chat, didn't stay long.

As time passed, Tommy's drink had not arrived. As luck would have it, Cy Marcus, the man who was believed to be the owner of Cy's, approached Tommy to say hello. I heard Tommy ask Cy, "Where's my fucking Dewar's and water?" I turned to look at Cy and saw the blood drain from his face, as if he'd seen a ghost. Cy turned and walked away very quickly and returned almost immediately with the Dewar's and water. It was in that moment that I knew for sure Tommy Ricciardi was the real thing. Tommy's comment upon receiving the drink from Cy wasn't, "Thank you," it was, "It's about time." Tommy's face had a scowl. Needless to say, Cy, whose face was still pale, didn't hang around for small talk with Tommy.

Around this same time, in my outward capacity as a Special Agent, I was in communication with a branch manager of a financial institution. I had served a grand jury subpoena on this bank and had to pick up the requested records as they were made available. The bank manager and I talked frequently when I visited the bank. I learned from him that he was a former FBI Agent who had left the Bureau to enter the private sector. He knew from conversations with me that I was interested in organized crime. During one of our conversations he told me that he lived directly next door to Tommy Ricciardi. He asked if I knew who Ricciardi was. I commented that I had heard the name, which was certainly an understatement. This guy advised me that Tommy's son regularly played with his son. He told me that he overheard conversations between the two boys.

During one occasion, the branch manager's son asked Tommy's son where his father was traveling. Tommy's son replied, "He's in San Diego." The branch manager said that the day after this exchange between the two boys, he read in the *Los Angeles Times* that Frank Bompensiero had been murdered gangland-style while in a phone booth engaged in a conversation. This hit on Bompensiero occurred on February 10, 1977.

Frank Bompensiero was alleged to be the head of the San Diego Mafia Family. He also was alleged to be an FBI informant. Rumor has it that he was on the phone with an FBI agent when Tommy shot him with his patented silencer equipped .22 caliber hand gun. This same weapon was believed to have been used in other Mafia "Hits". At the time that Bompensiero was shot while talking on the telephone, he probably was actually speaking with one of his Mafia colleagues who set him up for the murder. This guaranteed that he would be in the telephone booth at a certain time when the killer knew he would be there. Jimmy Fratianno confirmed this during his conversations with FBI agents. The Law of Omerta didn't apply to Jimmy, or Frank Bompensiero for that matter. Jimmy was given the moniker of "Jimmy the Weasel." He eventually went into the Witness Protection Program and then died of complications of Alzheimer's disease in Oklahoma in 1993. The so called Law of Omerta was the Mafia's code of silence; the rule prohibiting its members speaking about the Mafia or any of its activities, particularly with law enforcement. The Mafia dealt with "Rats" in a severe and permanent way; they were killed.

The bank manager related another conversation between the two boys whereby Tommy's son told his son that Tommy was in Las Vegas. The bank manager said that a short time later he learned of a gangland-style murder of two government witnesses who were in Las Vegas to testify in the trial of a Mafia figure.

According to *Hollywood Mafia Mobsters*, Tommy Ricciardi, aka TR, was an enforcer for the New York based Columbo Mafia Family before moving to Los Angels to become a member of the Los Angeles Mafia family headed up at that time by Dominic Brooklier.

Dominic's son, Anthony "Tony" Brooklier, was a prominent Los Angeles-based criminal defense attorney who represented his father, as well as other Los Angeles Mafia figures such as Michael

Rizzitello. I knew Tony Brooklier from my outward position as a special agent. This is just an example of why I wouldn't succeed in a deep cover operation in Los Angeles. Too many people in the business knew who I really was.

Many media sources have reported about the killing of Frank Bompensiero, including an article entitled "Footnotes On Assassination of Frank Bompensiero" that appeared in the *San Diego Reader* on February 10, 2018, written by Julie Stalmer. In March 1978, five organized-crime figures, including Ricciardi, were indicted for racketeering and the Bompensiero murder. The indictment and Bompensieros's murder were connected to an FBI undercover pornography sting operation. Tommy Ricciardi died of a heart attack in 1979, before the trial began. Tommy was known by media and law enforcement folks as the "Mafia hitman with a pacemaker." At the time of his death, Tommy Ricciardi was in a federal prison serving time for an extortion conviction.

I was finally introduced to the boss, Mike Rizzitello, by Vinnie, a bartender at Cy's. Vinny was from Buffalo, New York, and I was from Rochester, New York. So, Vinny and I had a geographic connection in addition to our joint Sicilian heritage. Vinny seemed to always be behind the bar at Cy's when I was there.

Mike Rizzitello was born in Montreal, Canada, but spent his formative years in New York City. He allegedly was aligned with the Jocy Gallo crime family. It was rumored that Rizzitello relocated to the Los Angeles area after he was involved in the Columbus Day hit on Joe Colombo. Another law enforcement theory was Rizzitello was sent out to the Los Angeles area to organize the local Mafioso who were all trying to be the boss. According to public record sources, after moving to California Mike Rizzitello was convicted of armed robbery in 1962 and spent nine years in prison. He was released in 1971, but later convicted of fraud in 1976. Three other criminal trials ended with acquittals. His last conviction was in 1988 for attempted murder.

The attempted murder case pertained to one of Mike Rizzi's so-called legitimate business endeavors that involved his association with the Mustang Club, a topless bar located in Santa Ana, California. According to Silver Screen Wiseguys, Rizzitello wanted control over the entire establishment and its lucrative profits. At the time, Bill Carroll was the owner and financier for this establishment who Rizzi first met when they both were in State Prison in Chino, Calfiornia. After being given an offer from Rizzi that he couldn't refuse, Carroll actually did refuse the offer and was accused by Mike Rizzi of "not letting us eat" (this is a phrase that was used in one of the Godfather movies). Carroll was shot three times in the head on May 1, 1987. Rizzitello allegedly was the triggerman, while Joseph Grosso, a Rizzi associate, allegedly restrained Carroll.

Mike Rizzitello used Cy's Rubio Lounge as a place to hold court. Rizzitello, as well as those who associated with him, were always under surveillance by law enforcement at all levels. It was not uncommon for Rizzitello to enter Cy's with a parade of law enforcement officers right behind him. He knew who they were, so it was a bit of a game. Everyone knew who the players were.

On one occasion, a local hard hat named Tommy (not Ricciardi), who was well known at Cy's, was very drunk and got out of hand. Tommy sat at the bar about two stools away from me. Rizzitello was holding court with a few of his goombahs at his usual table in the back of the bar.

At one point, Rizzitello tired of Tommy's loud talk and confronted him. I heard Rizzitello say to Tommy "You're very drunk and making a fool of yourself. I want you to go home". Rizzitello also told Tommy that he shouldn't drive and that he, Rizzitello, would call a cab to take him home. Rizzitello actually asked Vinny to summon a cab to Cy's.

Within a few moments, a cab driver stepped into Cy's and asked, "Did anyone call for a cab?" Tommy rose from his stool and departed out the door with the cab driver. Inexplicably, he returned to Cy's a few minutes later however, and walked toward the bar stool that he had vacated.

Rizzitello was seated back at his table talking to a few other guys. From that vantage point, Mike Rizzi had an unobstructed view of the entrance to Cy's and saw Tommy come back inside. At this time also, a happy hour piano player tickled the ivories, playing Italian songs. Mike Rizzi loved Italian music and it was played frequently at Cy's when Mike was there. If memory serves, Bobby Marotta, another Buffalo transplant and friend of Vinny's, was playing the piano. He played Mike Rizzi's favorite Italian songs.

When Tommy walked in, Rizzi saw him and stood up. At that exact moment the piano player stopped playing. Vinny the bartender, seeing what was happening, stopped pouring a drink, in mid-stream. It seemed as if the liquid dripping from the bottle was suspended in mid-air. Like a scene from an old western movie when music was playing and people were talking and laughing until the bad ass walked in the bar and then everything stopped. That's what happened at Cy's that day.

Tommy headed for the bar stool. Mike Rizzi walked toward Tommy, like a defender in a football game trying to intersect with the ball carrier. Tommy was a big guy, but Rizzi was built like a linebacker. He was something north of six feet tall and at least two hundred and forty solid pounds.

All of this happened directly adjacent to where I was seated. As he approached Tommy, I heard Mike Rizzi say to him in a low voice, but loud enough that I could hear him, "What the fuck are you doing back here. I told you to leave. I called a cab for you. Why are you disrespecting me by coming back in here?"

Tommy began to cry uttering "I don't want to go home." Mike said to Tommy "Get the fuck out of here and don't come back until you're sober and can act like a gentleman."

Tommy left and did not return that day. Vinny looked at me from behind the bar and just shook his head. The key word here is respect. Mike demanded respect and virtually always received it. No one dared to show disrespect to Mike Rizzi.

Another time, I was in Cy's and it was raining very hard outside. A barmaid was getting ready to leave at the end of her shift, but she didn't have an umbrella or a jacket. I wore a coat into the bar that day and set it on the seat next to me. It was a London Fog coat that I purchased when I was detailed to Secret Service for dignitary protection assignments. The Secret Service guys wore London Fog coats when it was cold. They were very useful in hiding Uzis, 12-gauge shot guns, also known as "Tubes", and other firearms.

The barmaid began complaining to Vinny that it was raining outside and she didn't have a jacket or an umbrella. Vinny leaned over the bar toward me and said, "Al, why don't you be a gentleman and give this lady your coat. She'll return it, no problem" So that's what I did, I loaned my London Fog coat to the barmaid. After thanking me, she promptly departed wearing my coat.

Several weeks went by and the barmaid did not return the coat to me. In fact, I never saw the barmaid in Cy's again. I asked Vinny about the barmaid and my coat and Vinny said he didn't know what happed to her or my coat. This became a running gag between Vinny and me and whoever was in ear shot of Vinny when he would tell the story about me lending my coat to the barmaid and the barmaid running off with it. Vinny could always tell a funny story

One night when Mike Rizzi was leaving Cy's, as was his custom, on his way out he leaned over the bar to shake Vinny's hand. Rizzi's hand always contained cash, usually a one hundred dollar bill. He would give it to Vinny as a tip. and then would say to him in the Sicilian dialect "Sa benedica" This term is an old Sicilian respectful greeting used when saying goodbye or hello. It loosely means, "may god bless you". My father used this term when leaving a family gathering and saying goodbye.

As Mike shook Vinny's hand, Vinny said to Mike, "Just a minute. I want you to meet someone." He introduced Mike Rizzi to me. He told Rizzi that I was from Rochester, and that I was a good guy. He then related to Mike the story about the barmaid and my coat. Rizzi said, "Nice to meet you. Don't worry about the coat, kid, I'll make sure that you get your coat back." I never saw my London Fog again. So much for Mike Rizzi's clout.

A postscript to the Mike Rizzi saga involves another IRS-CID special agent who had to interview Terry Rizzitello, Mike Rizzi's wife, about a matter unrelated to Mafia business.

Terry Rizzitello worked at a legitimate business in some type of clerical position. The special agent had no idea who Mike Rizzi was. The agent returned to the IRS-CID office the day after his interview with Terry Rizzitello, which was conducted at the Rizzitello residence in Canoga Park, California. This special agent began talking to other agents about interviewing a lady named Terry Rizzitello. He said that while he was interviewing Mrs. Rizzitello at her home, her teenaged daughters swam naked in their pool.

The special agent described how the drapes were open and he could clearly see the young women cavorting around the pool while he was interviewing Mrs. Rizzitello. I overheard the story of the naked girls swimming in the pool. I entered the conversation and explained to the special agent that Terry Rizzitello was the wife of Mike Rizzi, the local Mafia boss, and the naked girls that he had viewed the night before were Mike's daughters. The special agent's face took on a look of concern and he never again left the office without his weapon.

While hanging out at Cy's, I met Bobby C. Bobby was fairly short and thin with jet black hair. He was a small-time wannabe who allegedly was involved in loan sharking and drug sales. Bobby was observed by me speaking with Mike Rizzi and some of Mike's associates who frequented Cy's so I wanted to talk with Bobby C in an attempt to gather information about Mike Rizzi and the others. I certainly had to be cautious as to how I broached the subject of

Mike Rizzi and his associates in conversation with Bobby C, but that's why I got paid the big money. I had a knack of obtaining information from people who ordinarily wouldn't provide that information, particularly to people they didn't know. And, it didn't hurt that folks at Cy's would constantly see me in conversation with Vinny, who was well respected and trusted.

Bobby and I had dinner on several occasions at Tony Roma's restaurant at the front end of the strip mall where Cy's was located. During one of the dinners, Bobby C told me that when he loans money he takes collateral in the form of trust deeds on property, pink slips on cars, or other valuables to secure his loans. He claimed that he didn't break anyone's legs if they failed to make their payments, he just foreclosed on property or repossessed vehicles. Somehow, I didn't quite believe him, though I never really pressed him about it. Bobby volunteered this during one of our conversations. He probably thought I might need a loan sometime. And, our conversations never approached the Mike Rizzi subject.

On one occasion when I was chatting with Bobby C. at Cy's, Frank Hronek, a veteran Organized Crime investigator for the Los Angeles County District Attorney's Office, came in. Hronek was a legend within the law enforcement community in that it was believed that he knew everything there was to know about the mafia element in Los Angeles. He had a reputation of having a large stable of informants who kept him updated on the activities of the local Mafia folks. He saw me sitting and chatting with Bobby C. Hronek knew me as an IRS-CID special agent but he didn't approach me. A day or two later, Hronek contacted me and asked what I was doing in the company of Bobby C. I couldn't tell Hronek about my undercover assignment. Hronek certainly understood but cautioned me that Bobby C. was a very dangerous person. Hronek stated that Bobby C. was known to beat people up to collect debts or to impress a girlfriend. I thanked Hronek for this cautionary information.

About one week later, while reading the morning newspaper, I read an article about a man who crashed his car into a fence at a used car lot, jumped out of his car, and then shot and killed a used car salesman. This activity apparently had nothing to do with a Lemon Law violation. The killer was identified as Bobby C. The article described how the used car salesman and Bobby C met at a party the evening prior to the shooting. The article described Bobby C as being very drunk and annoying everyone at the party. The used car salesman made the fatal mistake of throwing Bobby C. into the pool to sober him up. No good deed goes unpunished.

A postscript to my experiences at Cy's Rubio lounge began with Mike Rizzitello entering Cy's one day followed by the usual parade of law enforcement officers. Bringing up the rear of this parade were two ATF agents, dressed in tee shirts and jeans trying to look like they were not with the other law enforcement officers. They both took seats at the bar next to me. I knew these guys and they both knew me as an IRS special agent. However, they did not speak or even look at me. When I subsequently spoke to them, they thought that I was conducting surveillance and didn't want to burn me.

The two ATF agents each drank a beer and then eventually left. Almost immediately upon their departure, Vinny walked over to where I sat, leaned over the bar and said to me, "Who the fuck do those guys think they are. I can smell a cop a mile away." My retort to Vinny was "Those were cops??"

I later discovered that Cy Marcus was not the real owner of Cy's. The owner of record for Cy's was the mother of a then very prominent and successful NFL football player. I actually attended the same college at the same time with this NFL football player.

On October 26, 2005, Michael Rizzitello died of complications of cancer at the age of seventy-eight in Palm Springs, California. Most people who knew Mike Rizzi will remember him as a very powerful Mafia figure who commanded respect and could terminate someone's life if he so desired. From my perspective, his legacy will always be that although he was a very powerful Mafia figure, he could not arrange to have a barmaid return my London Fog to me.

CHAPTER

2

FROM COMPOSER
TO SCALPER

Ticket Scalping is the act of reselling tickets to events for an inflated cost, usually far above the original selling price. Scalping is successful in part because it can be a challenge to get tickets to the opening night of a highly touted Broadway play, the concert of a popular musical artist, or a Super Bowl game, unless a person is willing to pay an exorbitant amount to ticket brokers for those tickets or has an inside source. The law of supply and demand generated high prices on the "Secondary market" to obtain these tickets.

Legitimate ticket brokers can easily obtain tickets to most events through their connections within the event's ticket holders; whether that's season ticket holders who opt not to attend a certain event, or the event organizers. This is a story about Los Angeles based ticket brokers having access to unusually large numbers of tickets to the 1980 Super Bowl and how that access was made possible by a very inside source.

In the fall of 1983, the Los Angeles District, IRS Criminal Investigation Division received allegations that tickets to the 1980 Super Bowl, held at the Rose Bowl in Pasadena, California, had been scalped for an exorbitant fee.

I learned during this investigation that the National Football League distributes Super Bowl tickets to all of the NFL teams. Every team receives tickets that they can distribute as they see fit, either selling or giving them away. A formula provides for each participating team to receive more tickets than other teams. The host team, the NFL team in whose city the Super Bowl is held, also receives more tickets than other NFL teams. The Los Angeles Rams football team was not only a participating team, but it was also the host team for the 1980 Super Bowl. Since the Rose Bowl had in excess of one hundred thousand seats, it was estimated that the Rams may have received upwards of twenty-five thousand tickets to the 1980 Super Bowl.

The information received by L.A. CID alleged that Dominic Frontiere caused the 1980 Super Bowl tickets issued to the L.A Rams by the NFL to be removed from the custody of the Ram's Ticket Manager and transported to the residence of Dominic and Georgia Frontiere. At the time, Dominic Frontiere was the husband of the then owner of the Los Angeles Rams, Georgia Frontiere. The information further alleged that Dominic may have removed a substantial number of those tickets (estimated to be as many as five thousand) from the residence and then sold them to ticket brokers through an individual identified as RC.

Dominic Frontiere, in addition to being the husband of Georgia Frontiere, was a renown composer of music for TV shows and movies. He had successfully scored the themes for TV shows such as *The Rat Patrol, Outer Limits,* and *The Flying Nun.* He also scored the music for such movies as *Hang 'Em High, On Any Sunday,* and *The Stunt Man.* The initial information received about the scalping of tickets to the 1980 Super Bowl shined a light of suspicion on Dominic Frontiere as being responsible. He immediately became the composer who also was a ticket scalper.

RC-was a Secret Service asset. He had been caught up by the Secret Service in a counterfeiting operation. So, to avoid prosecution, he agreed to provide information to the Secret Service regarding the counterfeiting of US currency. The Secret Service in return agreed to not push for his prosecution if he continued to provide useful and credible information. The term "What have you done for me lately" underscored his continued freedom.

During my investigation, I obtained RC's name through a series of interviews with Los Angeles-based ticket brokers who had purchased tickets to the 1980 Super Bowl from RC and then sold them at very high prices. In addition to identifying RC as the source of the 1980 Super Bowl tickets, the ticket brokers provided documents that reflected how many tickets were obtained from RC and what RC was paid for those tickets.

I contacted RC to interview him and solicit his cooperation in our investigation. Here again, RC readily agreed to provide information about Dominick Frontiere and the scalping of 1980 Super Bowl Tickets if he was given assurances that he would not be prosecuted. He was given those assurances in return for his total and complete cooperation. And, he did cooperate in the ongoing investigation and he also agreed to testify, if necessary.

RC confirmed that he obtained the tickets to the 1980 Super Bowl from Dominic Frontiere and then sold those tickets to ticket brokers. He identified the ticket brokers who he sold the tickets to, the approximate number of tickets that he sold to each and the approximate amount of money he received from each ticket broker in return for providing the tickets. The information provided by RC regarding the sale of the tickets to ticket brokers reasonably agreed with the information obtained from those ticket brokers.

RC also confirmed that he gave the proceeds of the ticket sales, minus his cut, to Dominic. RC agreed to cooperate in the investigation by continuing to deal with Mr. Frontiere and then provide information to me generated from their interactions. This was necessary for a successful prosecution because we needed more than RC's word regarding how and from whom he obtained the tickets and what he did with the proceeds from the sales of those tickets. We needed recorded conversation between RC and Dominic wherein Dominic confirmed that he provided the tickets to RC and RC provided proceeds from the sales of those tickets to Dominic. RC had to cause this subject to come up during his conversations with Dominic during the course of our investigation. Dominic eventually provided to RC a written document detailing what he should tell investigators if he was ever interviewed regarding his sales of 1980 Super Bowl tickets.

RC confirmed that he regularly provided information to Secret Service Agents pertaining to the counterfeiting of United States currency. Professional curtesy required that I contact the Secret Service Agent who handled RC and advise that I was going to use RC for the Frontiere investigation. After some "Negotiations" that required the involvement of our Chief and the local Secret Service Special Agent in Charge (SAC), the Secret Service Agent did not stand in our way in using RC to assist in our investigation. In fact, Secret Service agents were instrumental in investigating and helping to successfully prosecute another individual who got involved in our investigation.

Special Agents with IRS Criminal Investigation routinely contact targets of investigations to advise those targets that they are under investigation. This provides the targets an opportunity to provide mitigating information that may explain what appears to be criminal conduct. Also, these interviews frequently provided agents with additional evidence of criminal conduct. Mr. Frontiere was contacted and advised that he was under investigation and that the investigation pertained to allegations relating to the sales of tickets to the 1980 Super Bowl. After this contact, Mr. Frontiere retained legal representation. Mr. Frontiere was subsequently interviewed in the office of his then attorney. The interview was recorded with the permission of Mr. Frontiere and his attorney. During this interview, Mr. Frontiere made certain statements and answered some questions in a manner that defied credulity.

Criminal defense attorneys who represent clients investigated by the Internal Revenue Service, Criminal Investigation Division, can request a meeting with the United States Department of Justice (DOJ), Tax Division to discuss their client's case. Unlike other violations of federal laws, DOJ, and specifically the Tax Division, must approve all prosecutions that include tax violations. Virtually all other violations of federal laws can be prosecuted with only the authorization of the United States Attorney in whose district the case will be handled.

On April 9, 1985, a meeting was conducted at the DOJ Tax Division offices in Washington, DC, to discuss the Frontiere case. Frontier's legal team, which included Steve Wilson and another defense attorney requested the meeting and they attended the meeting. The Government was represented by Roger Olsen, Deputy Assistant Attorney General for Criminal Tax; Richard Leon, a Senior Trial Attorney for the DOJ Tax Division assigned to the Frontiere case; Bruce Kelton, a Los Angeles Strike Force Attorney assigned to the Frontiere case; and me. I was the case agent for the Frontiere case.

Roger Olsen was a graduate of the University of California, Berkeley where he received a BA. He also received a JD from the Boalt Hall School of Law and an LLM from George Washington University. He was nominated by President Ronald Reagen to be the Assistant Attorney General for the Department of Justice Tax Division in 1986. After leaving the Tax Division, Mr. Olsen entered private practice where he specializes in tax matters.

Bruce Kelton was a Department of Justice attorney assigned to the Los Angeles Strike Force. The United States Organized Crime Strike Force was created in the late 1960's by an initiative promoted by the late Senator Robert F. Kennedy. Its purpose was to use resources from various law enforcement agencies (federal, state and local) in coordinated efforts to investigate traditional organized crime activities. There are several Strike Forces around the country and they operate independently from the United States Attorneys offices.

Bruce Kelton was the Deputy Chief of the Los Angeles Strike Force. Prior to becoming a US Department of Justice Attorney,

Bruce Kelton was an Assistant District Attorney in Manhattan for six years, specializing in homicide cases. Bruce was a career prosecutor. Bruce was and still is a very funny guy. He could have been successful as a standup comic. I recall that at the retirement ceremony of an IRS-CID group manager, Steve Allen, the famous entertainer, was in attendance and said a few words about his friend, the retiring group manager. Mr. Allen's presentation was after that of Bruce Kelton's. At the outset of Steve Allen's presentation, he mentioned that following Bruce Kelton was a tough act to follow. He said that Bruce was funnier than most of the comedians that he had worked with.

Richard Leon was a Senior Trial Attorney for the Department of Justice, Tax Division assigned to the Frontiere case. He is a graduate of Harvard Law School where he received a Masters of Laws degree. He also received a JD from Suffolk University of Law and a BA from the College of Holy Cross where he was a classmate of Supreme Court Justice Clarence Thomas. After leaving the Justice Department, Mr. Leon entered private practice with the Baker & Hostetler law firm and then moved over to Vorys, Sater, Seymour and Pease. In 2002 he was appointed by President George W. Bush to become a United States District Court Judge in the District of Columbia. At his "Investiture", Justice Leon was sworn in as a District Court Judge by Justice Thomas. In his "Spare time", Justice Leon was an assistant professor of law at St. John's University School of Law, and an adjunct professor at The George Washington University Law School and the George Washington University Law Center.

The purpose of the meeting at the DOJ, Tax Division was to discuss the Frontiere case and allow the attorneys for Mr. Frontiere to provide mitigating information–they thought would dissuade prosecution. That didn't happen. In fact, the Frontierie attorneys inadvertently provided substantiation of Dominic's handwriting on a document provided to RC by Mr. Frontiere. The document provided a line-by-line response that RC was to provide to government agents if he was contacted and questioned regarding how he obtained and sold tickets to the 1980 Super Bowl. I placed the document, written on a yellow legal-size paper, on the table, between me and one of the Mr. Frontiere's attorneys, who was seated directly across the table from me. I placed that document there purposely so that Dominic's attorneys would see it and know that we had it. I said nothing about this document but the ploy worked as one of Dominic's attorneys commented that the handwriting on the document was in fact Dominic's. This was what we needed because our handwriting expert could not conclusively say that the writing on the document was Dominic's when compared to known handwriting exemplars of Dominic.

I've always been a football fanatic, having played in high school, the military, and sand lot with guys who played in high school, college, and semi-pro. The athletes that I played sand lot with eventually formed a semi-pro team. However, because I had been recently commissioned as a special agent with IRS-CID, I didn't have the time to devote to practice and play games, so I didn't join them.

I also coached youth football for twenty-five years. So, football was in my blood. I loved professional football. Many of my childhood heroes were NFL football players like Jimmy Brown, Johnny Unitas, Sam Huff, and others.

It's always been the norm in the Criminal Investigation Division that the case agent would be involved in the most critical interviews, including interviewing the targets of the investigations and the accountant or accountants who maintained the books and records of that target or targets. The case agent would certainly be involved in the interview of the preparer of the tax return or tax returns that were at issue in the investigation. In fairly large investigations, interviews of less important witnesses would be assigned to other Special Agents.

I was less than thrilled when my group manager assigned all of the interviews of the owners and other officials of many National Football League teams to other Special Agents

These interviews were necessary to document how other teams handled their distributed share of 1980 Super Bowl tickets. It was explained to me that a general usually stays behind during battles to properly manage those battles. This explanation did not placate me, but it was what it was.

At the conclusion of the investigation, and with the approval of DOJ Tax Division, on June 19,1986, Dominic Frontiere was indicted for filing a false United States Income Tax Return because he did not report income earned from scalping tickets to the 1980 Super Bowl. The indictment also included a charge that he lied to Internal Revenue Service investigators during an interview.

The indictment of Dominic Frontiere would have garnered huge publicity. However, on the exact day that the indictment was announced, Len Bias, a standout basketball player for the

University of Maryland thought to be a very high draft pick for an NBA team died. His death was reportedly from a cocaine-induced heart attack. The media coverage pertaining to the death of Len Bias was extreme and left little room for media coverage of the indictment of Dominic Frontiere.

On October 22,1986, Dominic Frontiere pled guilty to filing a false Federal Income Tax Return and to lying to Internal Revenue Service investigators. Frontiere was subsequently sentenced to serve one year and one day in prison and fined fifteen thousand dollars. He was also placed on probation for a period of three years after serving his prison sentence. Implicit with convictions for criminal tax violations is an order to cooperate with the Internal Revenue Service so that appropriate tax liability and associated interest and penalties can be assessed for the year or years of conviction.

Mr. Frontiere died in December 2017.

During the course of this investigation, one of Dominic Frontiere's good friends, H. Daniel Whitman, aka Danny Whitman, got wind of RC's intent to cooperate with the government in its investigation of Mr. Frontiere. In an effort to help his friend, he decided to hire a hitman to kill RC. We ultimately learned that it was Whitman who originally introduced Dominic Frontiere to RC as a source who could help Mr. Frontiere scalp the tickets to the1980 Super Bowl. Whitman owned and operated a restaurant called Cyrano's, located on the trendy Sunset Strip, in Hollywood, California

Through confidential informants we learned that Whitman had plans to hire a hitman to kill RC, so we helped Whitman find an appropriate hit man. Unfortunately for Whitman, the person that was steered in his direction and who ultimately helped him identify an appropriate hit man was an FBI informant who also knew Whitman. In short order, Whitman was introduced to a hitman, who happened to be an FBI undercover agent. Whitman and the "Hitman" cut a deal to kill RC. The hitman was required to provide proof to Whitman that RC was dead.

One of our Secret Service colleagues, Jerry Petievich, arranged to have a Hollywood makeup artist cause RC to appear as if he had been shot and killed. Polaroid photos of RC appearing to be dead were taken by Secret Service agents and provided to the undercover "Hitman".

Jerry Petievich is a best-selling author, having written *To Live and Die in L.A.*, *Money Man*, *The Sentinel*, *To Die in Beverly Hills*, and other novels. *To Live and Die in L.A.*, *Boiling Point* (published as *Money Man*), and *The Sentinel* were made into motion pictures. In addition to the Frontiere case, Jerry and I worked on some dignitary protection details together while he was still with Secret Service.

On December 6, 1983, the hitman met up with Whitman during the evening hours at Cyrano's, Whitman's Sunset Boulevard restaurant. The "Hitman" was wired for sound, wearing a recording device (Nagra) and a transmitter for safety and so that the agents monitoring this meeting from outside of Cyrano's can hear what's happening. During the meeting, the hitman told Whitman that he had killed RC and showed the Polaroid photos to Whitman that depicted RC supposedly dead.

After seeing the photographs, Whitman began talking about RC in the past tense. During the entire exchange between the

FBI Undercover Agent and Whitman in Whitman's restaurant, by total coincidence the theme from the Godfather was playing in the background—a little light dinner music. Dominic Frontiere, the renowned composer, could not have scored this meeting any better.

Whitman was arrested immediately after the meeting and after the hitman had departed. The entire meeting was not only recorded but it was observed by several special agent teams who were inside the restaurant eating dinner, and many more special agents—IRS-CID, FBI, and Secret Service—outside of the restaurant ensuring that Whitman would not leave the scene without being arrested.

No information was ever developed indicating that Mr. Frontiere had knowledge of Danny Whitman's plan for RC to be killed. With friends like that, Dominic did not need enemies.

H. Daniel Whitman was ultimately charged on December 8, 1983, with plotting to murder a witness in the probe of the 1980 Super Bowl tickets scalping matter. Whitman was first convicted on four counts, including conspiracy to murder and conspiracy to deprive a witness of his civil rights. This conviction was overturned on a technicality. On July 18, 1986, he was again convicted of conspiracy to kill a witness in a federal investigation. This conviction occurred in the courtroom of US District Court Judge Francis Whelan. In August 1986, Judge Whelan sentenced Whitman to eight years in prison and fined him ten thousand dollars. After serving out his prison sentence, Danny Whitman relocated to Conroe, Texas where he died in May 2017

There were several pre-trial hearings before Judge Whelan pertaining to the Whitman matter. During one of the pre-trial hearings, a series of Government Agents attempted to testify, and

Judge Whelan unceremoniously dismissed each agent prior to the conclusion of their testimony for reasons that I didn't quite understand. But, since we were in Judge Whelan's courtroom, we had to play by Judge Whelan's rules. To say Judge Whelan was a bit odd minimized his peculiarities. For example, prior to a Whitman hearing, Whelan held a hearing pertaining to a civil suit relating to injuries caused by a cable that snapped at the Long Beach Shipyard. Several employees working at the shipyard sustained life-threatening injuries. One of those employees was in the courtroom for the hearing, seated in a wheelchair as he could not walk on his own. One of his legs had been severed and the other severely injured when the cable broke loose.

When the lawyer representing that plaintiff made his appearance at the lectern, he mentioned that his client was present in the courtroom. Then he described his client's life-threatening injuries. Judge Whelan said, "I know all that, I want to know what the permanent injuries are."

Upon hearing this, I turned to Bruce Kelton, the Strike Force attorney who was assigned to both the Dominic Frontiere case and the Danny Whitman case and asked "Is Whelan going to preside over the Whitman case?" Kelton answered "I'm afraid so." Apparently, Judge Whelan had a severe hearing impairment and he was too vain to wear a hearing aid, so it seems that he didn't hear the attorney correctly.

I was called to testify for the government during a pretrial hearing in front of Judge Whelan pertaining to the Whitman matter. My testimony had to do with the fact that I was engaged in an official investigation pertaining to the scalping of tickets to the

1980 Super Bowl and that RC was a witness in that investigation. My testimony also covered my attempt to interview Whitman and Whitman's refusal to be interviewed citing that he had to go to work, and he wanted to have his attorney present.

Bruce Kelton cautioned me not to mention that Whitman refused to be interviewed because he wanted his attorney present. I'm not sure why but apparently Judge Whelan takes issue with this type of testimony. Perhaps it would be considered prejudicial as a jury may assume that Whitman was guilty because he wanted his attorney to be present during an interview. During my direct testimony, I mentioned that I did attempt to interview Whitman, but he refused to be interviewed. When asked why Whitman did not want to be interviewed, I indicated that he said that he had to go to work.

Jim Twitty was a prominent criminal defense attorney who represented Daniel Whitman. Twitty also represented Jack Catain, who was reported to have links to organized crime and who was also suspected of being involved in the ticket scalping case.

In his earlier years as an attorney, Mr. Twitty was also a government attorney assigned to the Los Angeles Strike Force for a period of time. During cross examination, Twitty pounded away at me to testify about the other reason Whitman did not want to be interviewed. I bobbed and weaved away from those questions and continued to look at Bruce Kelton seated at the prosecution table who shook his head confirming that I should not mention that Whitman wanted to have his attorney present during an interview.

Eventually, I testified that the other reason Whitman did not want to be interviewed was because he wanted his attorney present during the interview. I hardly got the words out of my mouth when Judge Whelan began to lambast me regarding that line of testimony, asking me how long I've been a special agent and that I should know better. Judge Whelan immediately kicked me off the witness stand and out of his courtroom. His last words to me were that I was to remain within thirty minutes of his courtroom in the event that I had to appear again.

Subsequent to the above-described hearing, I was assigned as the team leader to execute a search warrant at the residence of a known international narcotics trafficker. Special agents with the Drug Enforcement Administration advised that the trafficker was actually in Colombia and would not be at the residence when we executed the search warrant.

After announcing our presence, my team and I entered the residence. The lower level of the residence where we made entry contained several bedrooms. I directed several agents to search the bedrooms and detain anyone in those bedrooms for interviews.

Frank Day, a US Customs Special Agent, and I ran up the stairs to the upper level. The upper level contained the living room, kitchen, and another bedroom. When Frank and I reached the top of the stairs, the door to the bedroom opened and a large male figure appeared in the doorway. He occupied the entire doorway.

Frank and I drew our weapons. While Frank shouted, "Step out of the bedroom," I shouted "Don't move." The individual attempted to comply with both commands, doing a two-step. His left hand was hidden behind the door jam, so we couldn't see if his left hand held a weapon. We also observed a baby in a playpen directly behind the man. I hoped this guy didn't do anything stupid because we would have a hard time discharging our weapons with a baby in the line of fire.

Eventually, he showed his empty left hand and came out of the room. We were able to search and handcuff him and then place him on a couch. It turns out that this person was the international narcotics trafficker that DEA advised was in Colombia.

After securing the residence, as team leader I called into our command post and advised that we had made entry, secured the location, and were beginning to conduct the search and interviews.

During this call, a Branch Chief at CID advised me that I was wanted in Judge Whelan's courtroom and instructed me to assign another person to manage the search and get back to Judge Whelan's courtroom as quickly as possible.

My raid attire was not courtroom worthy, so I immediately went back to my office where I kept a suit, dress shirt, and tie. I changed into my courtroom attire, locked my weapon in a secure cabinet, and then I ran over to Judge Whelan's courtroom.

The United States Courthouse that housed Judge Whelan's courtroom sat directly across two busy streets from the Federal Building where my office was located so it took me a while to get to Judge Whelan's courtroom. Upon arriving in the vicinity of Judge Whelan's courtroom and knowing all witnesses had been excluded from the courtroom during the hearing unless they were testifying, I took a seat in the witness waiting room waiting to be called.

A short time after I arrived, a recess was called, and Jim Twitty approached me to ask where I had been. I explained that I was out on a raid and got back to the courthouse as fast as I could. The hearing resumed shortly thereafter, but only for a few minutes before another recess was called.

This time, Bruce Kelton approached me and asked what I had said to Twitty. I related our conversation. Bruce then told me that Twitty advised Judge Whelan that he had spoken to me just prior to the hearing resuming and that I told him that I was home sleeping before I came to the courthouse and that I really didn't want to hurry to get to the courthouse, or words to that effect.

I didn't know it at the time, but Adam Dawson, an investigative journalist and now a private investigator, was standing directly behind me when I talked with Twitty and remained behind me while I was talking with Kelton. Dawson overheard my conversation with Twitty. He interceded in my conversation with Kelton and confirmed to Bruce what I had said to Twitty. Bruce said to me just before heading back into the courtroom to continue with the hearing, "I'll take care of Twitty for you, Al."

Thirty minutes later, the hearing recessed a third time and Bruce approached me again and said that he had handled the Twitty matter for me. He said that Twitty had been objecting incessantly to certain matters during the hearing and at one point out of frustration, Judge Whelan admonished Twitty and told him that if he objected one more time, he would be held in contempt, Bruce responded to Judge Whelan's admonition by saying "That will be the day."

Due to his hearing impairment, Judge Whelan, thought that Twitty made that statement and held him in contempt of court.

Bruce took care of Twitty for me.

Although the Frontiere case was completed, as was the Danny Whitman matter, my interaction with Steve Wilson, one of Dominic Frontiere's attorneys, did not end.

ONE OF THE BEST THIEVES IN NEW ENGLAND

Every case seems to have some unique issues, at least most every case that I worked on. The Mondavano case was no different. This case introduced me to an author who I always wanted to meet because of the subject matter for which he specializes. This case also introduced me to an unforgettable character who was at one time a force in American politics. Both of these folks are an integral part of this chapter.

I'd been assigned to the Los Angeles Strike Force for a few months. I had just completed my work on the Frontiere case, which involved the "Scalping" of tickets to the 1980 Super Bowl and an attempt to kill one of our key witnesses. I was about to embark on the Barry Minkow ZZZ Best case when I received a telephone call from Steve Wilson, who was a member of the Frontiere defense team. Steve is a former Assistant United States Attorney (AUSA) who left that job to become a partner in a well-known boutique law firm that specializes in civil and criminal tax matters. I knew Steve for many years, having worked some criminal cases with him when he was an AUSA. He is now a United States District Court Judge in Los Angeles.

When I initially answered Steve's call, he began singing. I can say that Steve and I knew each other fairly well and he was a bit of a jokester and loved to sing, but always professional and represented his clients with great vigor and integrity. I thought to myself that the Frontiere case was over and I couldn't imagine why Steve Wilson wanted to speak with me. He advised that his call was not about the Frontiere matter but it was about another matter. He explained that he represented an individual named Dolly Ford, a travel agent who had become the victim of a fraud; a Ponzi scheme. Steve identified the fraudster as Danny Mondavano and he suggested that I speak with Ms. Ford about the matter. This telephone call from Steve Wilson was what launched the Danny Mondavano Ponzi Scheme case.

I didn't know it at the time of the telephone call from Steve Wilson, but during subsequent research I learned that Mondavano was on parole resulting from a stolen securities conviction that occurred on the east coast. He had been convicted of this crime more than once. Mondavano relocated to the Los Angeles area while still on parole and subsequently initiated a Ponzi scheme. Being fairly knowledgeable about traditional organized crime matters and having a very large personal library of organized crime books, I discovered that Mondavano was mentioned in Vincent Teresa's book, _My Life In The Mafia._ Teresa, once a heavy hitter in the New England Mafia Family, became a government informant.

He described his illegal activities with Danny Mondavano in his book. So, I began to learn about Danny Mondavano.

Mandavano became Vincent Teresa's best friend, and his partner in many illegal activites. Mondavano and Vincent Teresa were involved in a multitude of scams. In his book, Teresa advised that Mondavano was the most valuable property in his stable of hustlers indicating that they worked dozens of deals together, all of them profitable. Teresa said that Mondavano was a street thief, a swindler with a glib tongue and a flair for making money. Teresa is also credited with describing Mondavano as one of the best thieves in New England. Teresa described how he and Mondavano organized gambling junkets to Antigua, the Bahamas, London, and Las Vegas. They also operated crooked card games fleecing gamblers out of millions of dollars. They also were involved in moving stolen securities. The exact scheme that Mondavano used in his Ponzi operation and that was the subject of our investigation, was also carried out by Teresa long before Mondavano initiated his illegal activities in Southern California.

I subsequently interviewed Dolly Ford. Her story of Mondavano's Ponzi scheme was exactly the same as all of the other victim/witnesses that I ultimately interviewed. It also seemed to be a carbon copy of Teresa's scheme. The transactions with Mondavano were all in cash, he paid a high rate of interest (2% per week) for the funds invested with him and he paid the victims interest for their investment on a weekly basis, every week, until he didn't. Many victims of Mondavano's Ponzi scheme elected, at Mondano's suggestion, to not receive every weekly interest payment but instead "Rolled over" their interest payments into their principal investment, thus increasing the amount of money for which interest is earned; theoretically earning interest on interest. Also, this allowed Mondavano to kick the can down the road regarding making interest payments to victims who chose to "Roll over" their interest payments into their investment principal. Mondavano also offered victims an incentive to earn more money by introducing other investors to him. He would share the "Income" generated by the invested funds with those who introduced other investor/victims to him. He also offered what he termed "Ice cream deals". These were investments of the same nature but paid a higher rate of interest.

And how were the invested funds supposed to be used to earn income? Mondavano told his investors that he was lending invested funds to operators of "Flea Market" concessions so that they could buy product to sell. His story included that those folks could not get loans from traditional lending institutions, so they turned to the "street" to provide the funds. He said that he was loaning money to these folks at a high rate of interest; he effectively was a loan shark if he indeed did loan out the funds invested with him, which he probably did not. It seemed to make sense to those who "Invested" with Mondavano. Mondavano's pitch to "Investors" included that all of the transactions would be in cash so that the IRS could not become aware of, identify, and/or trace the funds that were being transacted, including the interest paid to the investors by Mondavano, which would ordinarily be reportable income to the investors. This aspect of Mondavano's pitch to prospective investors clearly resonated with them. Greed is a great motivator for fraud victims.

During the course of the investigation, I was led to an individual named Roy Elson. Mr. Elson, who is now deceased, became a fountain of information; a so-called "Gift that kept on giving". Roy Elson was, in his earlier life, the key aide to the late Senator Carl Hayden. Also, Elson ran unsuccessfully for the US Senate on two occasions. The first time he lost out to Paul Fanin and the second time he was beaten by Barry Goldwater. Carl Hayden was a very powerful Senator and so it was said that Elson, as Senator Hayden's key aide, had more political influence than most members of congress. After his stint with Senator Hayden, Elson became a lobbyist, cashing in on his contacts on "The Hill".

Elson was eventually introduced to Mondavano and his "Investment" program by a friend who invested with Mondavano and apparently initially earned substantial returns on her investment. Elson met with Mondavano and subsequently decided to invest funds with Mondavano after he observed his friend receive from Mondavano timely and substantial cash interest payments on her investment. Elson then began to approach some of his clients as well as some of his contacts on "The Hill" to invest in Mondavano's scheme. Elson became an integral part of the scheme by introducing many investors to Mondavano and becoming a conduit through which funds were invested and payments from Mondavano back to those investors were made. Elson became a "Middleman" between investors and Mondavano and earned money from Mondavano for being the "Middleman", in addition to earning interest from Mondavano on his personal investment. There came a time when all payments from Mondavano stopped and all investors who still had funds with him lost their investment. Mr. Elson and all of the investors that he convinced to invest with Mondavano were no exception. They lost all of the funds invested with Mondavano, either directly or through Elson.

Mondavano perpetrated the classic Ponzi scheme. This is a form of fraud whereby a fraudster lures investors with promises of earning large profits on their investments. Mondavano's pitch to investors regarding their investments also included the provision that all transactions would be in cash, beyond the view of the Government and thus the IRS would not know about the investments or profits they earned. The operators of Ponzi schemes never really use victim funds as represented to the investors or use very little of the victim's funds for such purposes. The funds generated by investors are generally used by the fraudster for personal expenditures; purchases of real property, high end automobiles, boats, planes, travel, etc. Mondavano was no different in the use of the investor's funds. The funds to make interest payments to earlier investors were then generated by funds invested with Mondavano by newer investors. In order for a Ponzi scheme to continue, new investors must continually be introduced into the scheme so that their funds can be used to make interest payments or fund withdrawals to earlier investors. Investor requests for withdrawals of principal are usually frowned upon by fraudsters who come up with various and sundry reasons why an investor should not or could not withdraw principal funds. When new investors are no longer introduced to the scheme, the Ponzi scheme dies a natural death and all payments to investors by the fraudster cease. The investors are then left holding an empty bag; no interest payments and their principal investment(s) gone.

Mondavano eventually stopped making payments to investors and stopped being available for contact.

Charles Ponzi has been credited with perpetrating the first Ponzi scheme in the 1920s. However, Sara Howe actually perpetrated the first recorded Ponzi type scheme in the late 1800s. They both were from Boston, as was Daniel Mondavano and Vincent Teresa. A coincidence I'm sure...

I attempted to contact Roy Elson on several occasions. I left telephone messages for him. About the time that I thought that I would never hear from Elson, the telephone rang and it was him. He started his telephone conversation with me with "I heard that you're looking for me". We then agreed to meet in person in Los Angeles.

The first time I met Elson in person, he was staying at the Biltmore Hotel in downtown Los Angeles. The Biltmore Hotel is an old and prestigious hotel that first opened its doors in 1923. At the time, it was the largest hotel West of Chicago. The interior of the hotel is very ornate, with decorated ceilings and fine art decorated wall coverings.

I met with Elson in his room at the Biltmore Hotel, along with another Special Agent, for the purpose of interviewing him regarding the Mondavano matter. Upon entering Mr. Elson's hotel room, he opened a suitcase that was the size of a steamer trunk. The suitcase contained literally hundreds of micro-cassette audio tapes as well as hundreds of legal-size yellow notepads. Mr. Elson explained that he recorded all of his telephone calls, all of them, including his telephone calls with Danny Mondavano. He said that he also made copious notes on the legal pads of all meetings in which he participated, including meetings with Mondavano. The notes were made contemporaneously with the conduct of meetings. Mr. Elson explained that he has recorded all telephone calls and made contemporaneous notes of all meetings since he was the key aide to Senator Carl Hayden. That's just what he did. As you might imagine, I was blown away by the way Mr. Elson documented his activities, including and particularly his contacts with Mondavano. This certainly added specificity and credibility to what Elson would verbally relate to me. It's actually illegal to record telephone conversations without specific approval from all parties to those telephone conversations. Some states require only approval from one participant in telephone conversations. The approving participant could actually be the person that is recording the conversation. This would make recording of telephone conversations legal. No matter, since Elson wasn't directed by law enforcement to record telephone or other conversations, the recordings could be used as evidence. I did caution him not to record any conversations going forward.

The details of this investigation are not essential to recite in this chapter but suffice it to say that Mr. Elson was the linchpin upon which the Mondavano case hung. He introduced me to many, many investor victims of the Mondavano Ponzi scheme, some of whom invested through Elson and some who invested directly with Mondavano. Many of the investor victims were United States government employees.

While the Mondavano investigation was ongoing, I was promoted to Group Manager and became a Supervisory Special Agent. I had to divest myself of cases assigned to me and have them assigned to other Special Agents. So, instead of actually working cases, I now was directing and supervising investigations. The Mondavano case was no different and it was assigned to SP, a superb Special Agent who continued the investigation and carried the matter through to a successful prosecution. Suffice it to say that Mr. Mondavano, his son Dennis, and his wife Rose were charged with a litany of federal criminal violations and ultimately convicted of these crimes.

At some point during the course of this investigation I was contacted by James Bamford, a New York Times bestselling author. Mr. Bamford is the author of several books pertaining to the National Security Agency (NSA). I obtained and read all of his books and they are a part of my personal library. At the time that Mr. Bamford contacted me, I had read his seminal book pertaining to the NSA entitled *The Puzzle Palace.* This was the first book that he authored about the NSA. He subsequently authored two other books about the NSA, *Body of Secrets* and *The Shadow Factory*. He also authored *A Pretext for War*, a book about 9/11 and the war in Iraq. He most recently authored *Spyfail*. Coincidences being what they are, I was assigned to one of the military arms of the NSA when I was in the Air Force, so I was quite familiar with the material that Bamford presented in *The Puzzle Palace* (as well as in his subsequent books about the NSA). However, I was baffled as to how Bamford was able to obtain all of the information that appeared in his NSA books since I always believed that this material was highly classified. In addition to authoring books, he has written articles for Foreign Policy Magazine, The Nation, The Wall Street Journal, and more. He also is a contributor to many electronic news media outlets as well as creating material for PBS. Also, he was an Investigative Producer for ABC's World News Tonight with Peter Jennings. It goes without saying that I always wanted to meet Jim Bamford.

When Jim Bamford contacted me, he didn't want to talk about the NSA. He wanted to talk to me about Danny Mondavano. Apparently, he had been in contact with Roy Elson and Elson provided him with my name and contact information. What I didn't know at the time but subsequently came to learn is that Elson had knowledge of other matters that ultimately became the subject of Federal Strike Force investigations and prosecutions. As it relates to the Mondavano matter, Elson evidently contacted some Los Angeles/Palm Springs area Mafia figures in what turned out to be a misguided effort to engage them to help him recover funds that were lost to Mondavano. Elson knew of Mondavano's connection to Organized Crime figures and felt that he could convince some of the local Mafia folks to help him. As you might imagine, this didn't work out too well for Elson. So, he had to go "On the lamb" attempting to avoid the Mafia. Roy lived in a camper for some time, moving about from place to place and having a weapon always at the ready. Bamford authored an article for the _Los Angeles Times_ entitled Taking On The Mob in which he detailed Elson's efforts to avoid the mob, the Mondavano Ponzi scheme, and other matters for which Elson got involved. So, his call to me was to gather information for his article. I wasn't able to provide much information because of restrictions on disclosures pertaining to our investigations. But, we did meet in person and ultimately began a friendship and professional relationship that endures to this day.

Although it didn't seem to Elson that his contacts with the local Mafia folks got him any closer to getting Mondavano to return the money that he took from Elson and others, it seems that behind the scenes the local Mafia boys were going to do something to Mondavano. Craig Anthony Fiato, usually referred to as Anthony, and his brother, Larry, were fringe Mafia associates who worked closely with some of the local family guys. They also worked closely with Bobby (Puggy) Zeichick, who has been described as an associate of the Los Angeles Mafia family. Zeichick in fact gave Anthony Fiato $1,000,000 to "Put on the street" in a loan sharking operation. Also, sources advised that Zeichick, Fiato and other associates organized local bookmakers and loan sharks to assist in their loan sharking activities.

According to Anthony Fiato, he and his brother met at Luigi Gelfuso's Encino apartment on May 17, 1984. Luigi Gelfuso was believed to be a "Soldier" in the Los Angeles Mafia family. Apparently, Gelfuso spoke privately with Anthony in the back bedroom of the apartment. Gelfuso told him to make a move on Danny Mandavano and gave him a photograph of him with a piece of paper with Mandavano's address. Gelfuso allegedly instructed Fiato to beat him to a pulp for owing $468,000. Fiato went to Mandavano's home but learned that he no longer lived there.

Also during this same time period, Mondavano contacted Elson and complained that he had been called on the carpet by Mafia folks regarding his Ponzi operation. He apparently knew that Elson had contacted some local Mafia folks. Mondavano told Elson that he caused him a great deal of harm and he (Mandavano) may be ordered to a "sit down" with local Mafia bosses. No information has been developed indicating whether or not Mondavano actually had this "Sit down", but he certainly did not return Elson's money.

In April 1988 Mondavano was indicted on several criminal charges resulting from his operation of the Ponzi scheme. Also indicted were his son, Dennis, and his former wife, Rose. Daniel Mondavano was "In the wind" after being indicted. In an effort to capture Mondavano, Special Agents from the Los Angeles and Phoenix Arizona CID offices began a comprehensive surveillance of Dennis Mondavano, Daniel's son who had moved to the Phoenix area. Apparently, a very close friend of Daniel Mondavano also moved to the Phoenix area, so he was also the subject of surveillance activity. It was felt that Daniel Mondavano would at some point travel to Phoenix to visit his son and/or his friend. Within a few days of the initiation of the surveillance activities in Phoenix, Mondavano's good friend was surveilled to the Phoenix airport where Daniel Mondavano was observed departing from the airport terminal and entering his friend's vehicle. A "Felony" car stop was initiated and Daniel Mondavano was arrested. Subsequently, Dennis and Rose Mondavano were also arrested.

On June 14,1988 Daniel Mondavano pled guilty to one count of conspiracy and two counts pertaining to criminal tax violations. Dennis Mondavano pled guilty to one conspiracy count. Rose Mondavano pled guilty to one criminal tax violation pertaining to filing a false income tax return for the 1983 tax year. Daniel Mondavano was sentenced to serve 5 ½ years in prison. Dennis Mondavano was sentenced to serve 4 years in prison, and Rose Mondavano was sentenced to serve 60 days in prison and to perform 2,000 hours of charitable work. All three were also sentenced to serve terms of probation (IE..Supervised Release) after completing the prison terms.

The docket for the above referenced criminal case reflects that on August 19, 1995 Judge Manuel Real issued a Bench Warrant for the arrest of Daniel Mondavano pertaining to allegations of violating the terms of his probation. The docket further reflects that on March 24, 2003 the bench warrant was returned unexecuted because it was determined that Daniel Mondavano was deceased, No additional details were made available.

The Revenue Agent

During the course of the Mondavano investigation, we learned that an IRS Revenue Agent had prepared income tax returns for Daniel Mondavano. Since this person is still alive and seemingly paid his debt to society, I will refer to him as "Bill A". He was a Revenue Agent for a period of time but then resigned his position with the IRS to initiate a private tax practice. It was during this time, while operating his private tax practice that he met Daniel Mondavano and began to prepare income tax returns for him. The tax returns that were prepared by "Bill A" and filed with the IRS underreported income earned by Mondavano, particularly the income he earned operating his Ponzi scheme. Also, the tax returns that were prepared by "Bill A" did not accurately identify the source of the income that was reported.

There came a time when "Bill A" returned to work as a Revenue Agent for the IRS. As such, he was not allowed to prepare tax returns as a business venture; certainly a conflict of interest.

However, while once again working as a Revenue Agent, "Bill A" prepared all of the underlying schedules from which Mondavano's tax returns could be prepared and he then provided those schedules to another tax preparer whose name appeared on Mondavano's tax returns as the preparer. The information provided by "Bill A" to be used to prepare Mondavano's tax returns by the other tax preparer also underreported Mondavano's true income and did not accurately identify the source of the income that was reported.

It is my understanding that "Bill A" ultimately entered into a plea agreement with the Government agreeing to provide information about Mondavano and testify, if necessary, at his trial. "Bill A" was let "Off the hook" in return for cooperating against Mondavano.

NARCOTICS MONEY LAUNDERING

CHAPTER

4

OPERATION BENDIX

The word Bendix has had different connotations over the years. There was a famous actor named William Bendix who starred in an early television sitcom called *The Life of Riley*. This chapter is not about him.

Then there's the Bendix Corporation. The Bendix Corporation is an American manufacturing and engineering company which has made automotive brake shoes, vacuum tubes, aircraft brakes, and other such products. The founder of this company was Vincent Hugo Bendix. This chapter is also not about that company or its founder. Then there was the Bendix washing machine. The Bendix washing machine was the first automatic washer with a full wash, rinse, and spin cycles. This washing machine was introduced at the Louisiana State Fair in 1937. This chapter is not about that specific washing machine either, but we're getting close to what this chapter is about.

This chapter is about the washing of money, to make dirty money generated via narcotics trafficking appear clean. This process is accomplished through a series of transactions, the first of which goes unreported, and the remainder are generally shrouded with false and misleading paperwork that serve to hide the true nature, source and ownership of the money.

In the spirit of total transparency, and to certainly give well-earned and well-deserved credit where credit is due, I was not the IRS-CID case agent on Operation Bendix. I was "E pluribus unum" on this case, as virtually every Special Agent in the Los Angeles District, Criminal Investigation Division office worked on this matter from time to time because of the complexities and the multiple investigative techniques used. It was manpower intensive, but well worth the human investment. However, I was more involved in this investigation than most of the Special Agents who participated.

One of the best and the brightest special agents was given the nod to handle Operation Bendix. Special Agent Dennis Dixon was assigned as the case agent to investigate the allegations presented below and to then steer this matter through the investigative phase and subsequent successful prosecution. Dennis began his career with the Internal Revenue Service in 1967 as a Revenue Agent, conducting tax audits. He transferred to the criminal investigative arm in 1969. Dennis's mantra was, "Work hard, play hard," and he indeed lived and looked the part, with his perpetual surfer like tan and athletic physique. He was a former Marine with the "Semper Fi" and can-do attitude.

The prosecution was handled by an assistant United States attorney (AUSA) who blazed the trail for the use of "Follow-the-money" techniques in investigating major narcotics trafficking organizations. And, who better to follow the money than the special agents of the IRS, Criminal Investigation Division? The Assistant United States Attorney assigned to this case was Robert J. Perry, who brilliantly guided the investigation to ensure that the maximum amount of evidence was gathered in an appropriate and court-worthy manner. Bob Perry was the lead counsel in the subsequent and successful prosecutions of those defendants who foolishly opted to tangle with him in the courtroom. Their choice to roll the dice and opt for a trial did not end well for those defendants. Bob Perry ultimately became a Los Angeles County Superior Court judge after leaving the US Attorney's office and then retired from the bench in March 2021. Perry also authored several books, including a book called *Dirty Money*, which presents and chronicles via his own experiences four major narcotics related investigations and prosecutions. All of the cases presented in Bob's book used the follow-the-money techniques and they all involve special agents with IRS, Criminal Investigation Division, as well as special agents of the Drug Enforcement Administration and the United States Customs Service. One of those cases is the subject of this chapter.

Operation Bendix involved a Los Angeles-based attorney who laundered tens of millions of dollars for major narcotics traffickers, and a bank that agreed to help him move the funds through its financial channels and not file the required Currency Transaction Reports. This service came with a price, however, in the form of fees paid to the bankers involved in the money laundering process. The price also included the life of one of the major participants in the money laundering process. As a result of this loss of life, we ended up hiding an undercover agent who we thought could also be at risk of being killed.

Nathan Markowitz was a former New York-based SEC attorney. He subsequently relocated to the Los Angeles area after leaving the SEC and was admitted to the California State Bar in April 1966. At one point in his legal career, he was a partner in a Beverly Hills-based law firm known as Sands & Markowitz where he took on SEC related case work. In about 1975, Markowitz joined with Harold Abeles to form Abeles and Markowitz. Both the Sands firm and the Abeles firm represented Defendants who were caught up in the Equity Funding fraud matter.

When Nathan Markowitz was associated with the firm founded by Leaonard Sands, Richard Sherman, a well-known criminal defense lawyer, was also associated with this firm. During his tenure at the Sands firm, Nathan Markowitz got involved in the representation of a Defandant who was caught up in the Equity Funding fraud. It was during this representation that Markowitz met Harold Abeles, whose firm was representing Julie Weiner, a principal of an accounting firm that served as the outside auditors for Equity Funding. Mr. Weiner, along with several other members of his firm were criminally charged in the Equity Funding fraud case.

Eventually, Markowitz left the Sands firm and joined Harold Abeles in his firm. As an aside, Harold Abeles was the biological father of Sara Gilbert and the adopted father of Melissa Gilbert, both actresses. Markowitz's tenure at the Ables firm didn't work out, so Markowitz struck out on his own and formed a sole practitioner firm known as Nathan Markowitz, Attorney at Law.

Although the exact timeframe is not known with any degree of certainty, during the mid to late 1970's Nathan Markowitz seemed to attract clients who were drug traffickers. He apparently had drug trafficking clients that were based in the Santa Barbara area.

It was well established by law enforcement that ships carrying loads of Marijuana and other illicit drugs would sit off the coast of Santa Barbara and small boats would then ferry the drugs from the ships to the shore where they were met by individuals in pickup trucks who would load their share onto the bed of the trucks and drive off. It was not uncommon for Markowitz and his wife to attend parties in the Santa Barbara area where the attendees included some of his drug trafficking clients. His clients were usually dressed in beach type attire at these parties while Nathan and his wife were dressed as if they were attending a formal cocktail party: Nathan in a suit and tie and his wife in a cocktail dress. They stood out from the crowd. Nathan was apparently always well dressed, but not ostentatious, at least during the mid 70's. He always wore a good suit, with a dress-shirt and tie. But, his style of dress was not considered worthy of being on the cover of GQ magazine. Nathan was described as being about 5 foot, eight inches tall, thin and he wore glasses. He apparently drove a Citroen Maserati. In the early eighties, when the IRS-CID criminal case was in process, Markowitz was known to wear more expensive clothing and flashy jewelry. This may be a testament to his success in providing money laundering services to the illicit narcotics trafficking community.

Nathan seemed to be sensitive about people knowing that he represented drug traffickers. He was once heard to complain that his reputation was being tarnished because rumors were circulating that he had drug traffickers as clients. However, when asked why he and his wife attended parties that were also attended by drug traffickers his answer was many of the attendees were his clients. So, his feelings regarding representing drug traffickers were complicated.

The Operation Bendix story began for IRS-CID in April 1980 with a tip from an individual who was in a unique position and had the proper prospective to learn about the possible money laundering activities of Nathan Markowitz. The tipster cannot and will not be further identified. Suffice it to say that the tipster was able to provide profoundly specific and accurate information that was very useful in crafting an investigative plan resulting in the successful prosecution of all of the those who participated in this money laundering scheme—all those that lived through the investigation and prosecution processes that is.

The tipster's information included that Markowitz set up foreign entities and related foreign bank accounts in the names of those entities, as a means of laundering large volumes of cash generated by major narcotics traffickers. The tipster also alleged that Markowitz was able to enlist the services of a local bank and its bankers to accept large amounts of cash generated by narcotics sales, enter that cash into the banking system, and move the funds to offshore bank accounts held in the names of foreign entities set up by Markowitz.

Garfield bank was identified by the tipster as the bank where large amounts of illicit cash began its journey in the Markowitz money laundering process. This financial institution had a few locations in the greater Los Angeles area including Montebello and Hollywood. The cash was delivered to Garfield Bank in the proverbial black bag and deposited to a Nominee account held at the bank. A Nominee account is a bank account held in the name of an entity or individual that is not the name of the actual owner of the funds on deposit. The cash deliveries to the Garfield Bank by Markowitz and his associates and the deposit of that cash to the nominee account were completed without the required filing of Currency Transaction Reports by the bank. This was part of the service provided by Garfield bank and its bankers to Markowitz for a fee.

Title 31 of the United States Code requires financial institutions to prepare and file with the United States Government Currency Transaction Reports (CTRs) on all cash transactions (deposits, withdrawals, purchases of money orders, wire transfers, etc.) that exceed ten thousand dollars. Ten thousand dollars and one cent would legally require a CTR to be prepared and filed. This requirement was part of the Bank Secrecy Act, a 1970 law created in part to prevent financial institutions from being used as tools by criminals (specifically Organized Crime organizations) to hide or launder ill-gotten gains. Money Laundering was not a crime at the time that this investigation was initiated. The actual money laundering law wasn't created until 1986. The term Bank Secrecy Act is an oxymoron because the provisions of this act required the reporting of certain transactions, the opposite of providing secrecy.

The tipster provided a picture of an attorney who was able to take large amounts of cash generated by illicit narcotics sales, introduce that cash into the banking system with the assistance of Garfield Bank and its bankers, and then move those funds offshore into foreign bank accounts held in the names of foreign business entities, including trusts that were established by Markowitz. The funds were then returned to the beneficial owners (narcotics traffickers) in the form of loans. Some of the funds were returned to the narcotics traffickers masked as wages so that the traffickers could report to the IRS income supposedly earned from legitimate sources that would support their lifestyle. This type of return to the traffickers required Markowitz to establish supposed legitimate business entities in the US to provide a source of legitimate income to the traffickers. All of this movement of funds occurred without the proper filings of reports that would have served to identify this activity.

One of the initial steps to confirm the information provided by the tipster was to research CTR filings to determine if any such filings were made by Garfield Bank pertaining to cash transactions executed by Markowitz. There were CTRs filed by Garfield Bank pertaining to transactions carried out by other customers but none relating to the Markowitz transactions. This meant that one aspect of the allegations provided by the tipster was found to have merit.

Investigating this case would not be easy and initiating undercover and parallel surveillance activities were essential in gathering the necessary evidence that would serve to cause a successful prosecution of all of the people involved in this scheme. The first and most crucial task would be to determine a way to introduce an undercover agent to Nathan Markowitz. The second task was to select an appropriate undercover agent who could pass as a narcotics trafficker or someone who assisted in the money laundering process for narcotics traffickers. A "Tinkers-to-Evers-to-Chance" introduction story was created.

Dixon and his team were able to craft a story that included a referral to Markowitz by someone who was at least nominally known by him. This story had to withstand scrutiny if Markowitz checked it out. It apparently passed the smell test because not one, but two IRS-CID undercover agents and one DEA undercover agent were successfully introduced to Markowitz.

WP was selected as one of the IRS-CID undercover agents. WP was a seasoned undercover agent who had successfully infiltrated criminal organizations and developed sufficient evidence during his undercover activities to support successful prosecutions. WP was not someone who would be readily identified as a government agent. WP looked more like a businessman or a college professor. WP was somewhat paunchy in stature and looked like a retired grandfather type. More often than not he appeared in rumpled clothing.

A second undercover agent was also selected to serve as WP's driver and bodyguard. The second undercover agent looked the part of a very tough guy. He had the outward appearance of someone who you wouldn't want to cross.

After a few telephone conversations, Markowitz and WP agreed to meet at Markowitz's office, which was located on an upper floor of a bank building near the Los Angeles International Airport, at the corner of Century and Airport Boulevards. The building was similar to other commercial buildings in the area. It was light gray in color, with windows on all sides. The windows were divided with white horizontal strips of what appeared be plaster, spanning from the top of the building to the top of the first floor. The offices on the first floor of the building, including the bank and airline ticket offices, had doors leading to and from the boulevards, both Century and Airport. The building also had a rear entrance, directly off the building's parking lot.

In preparation for this and all subsequent meetings at Markowitz's office, as well as general surveillance of Markowitz and his office, a surveillance game plan had to be set up and surveillance agents had to be selected and assigned. As it turns out, surveillance activities pertaining to the Markowitz case were very labor intensive for which virtually everyone in the Los Angeles District Criminal Investigation Division office participated from time to time. In addition, special agents with the Drug Enforcement Administration (DEA) and the Customs Service were also involved in the surveillance activities. A permanent surveillance command post had to be established near the Markowitz law office to properly manage and direct the surveillance activities.

The bank building was located directly across Airport Boulevard from the Marriott Hotel. The Marriott contained rooms with windows that allowed a direct view of the Airport Boulevard side of the bank building as well as the building's parking lot directly behind the building. This was an open parking lot and not a parking structure. The parking lot surface was paved with dark-colored asphalt and it contained the standard concrete bumpers delineating the end of each of the approximately fifty parking spaces. The parking lot was sprinkled with strategically located trees in planters that broke up the otherwise monotonous asphalt look. Today, an Embassy Suites hotel occupies the space that was once a parking lot.

The security director of the hotel, who was a former law enforcement officer and understood our needs, was contacted by Dixon. He helped arrange for Dixon and his team to secure long term rental of rooms that provided a clear view of the bank building and the adjacent parking lot. The location of these rooms was almost too good to be true. There were no trees or bushes to obstruct the view of the bank building and associated parking lot. Only an occasional bus or eighteen-wheeler stopped at the traffic light would cause a momentary disruption of the view.

The next step in setting up the surveillance aspects of the investigation was to select a field manager to manage the surveillance operation. PT was tapped to manage the surveillance activities. PT is a former Marine tank officer who was well experienced in surveillance operations and an organizational genius. He was also assigned to the same CID group as Dixon, which made the selection easy. No group lines were crossed which meant no approval from another group manager and/or branch chief had to be obtained to use PT for the duration of Operation Bendix.

PT then began the process of setting up his surveillance team; at least the initial group of special agents to handle the surveillance activities. PT then began to identify other special agents within the Los Angeles District to provide surveillance support as needed. DEA and Customs special agents were also included in the mix. PT was a great believer in establishing a workable and plausible plan, as well as a backup plan and a backup to the backup plan so that there was never a lag in the surveillance process. Any lags could result in missed opportunities to gather evidence.

Another piece of the surveillance operation involved the use of a fixed surveillance point where surveillance agents could see surveillance targets. The main entrance to the bank building was actually in the back of the building, off the parking lot. Visitors to the bank and offices within the bank building could park their vehicles in the bank building parking lot and walk directly into the bank building. Although the windows of the hotel rooms provided a good view of the side of the bank building and the parking lot, they did not provide a view of the door to the building. Visitors to the bank building who parked in the parking lot could not be observed actually entering the bank building.

PT decided to employ the use of a surveillance camper to house surveillance agents to observe people parking their vehicles in the parking lot and then entering the bank building. The surveillance camper looked like any other camper. It was an older model Chevrolet pickup truck that had a cab-over camper shell, with a rear entry door. This vehicle reflected scars imposed on it by special agents who were unaccustomed to driving such a vehicle. The cab-over shell provided an immovable impediment to parking this vehicle in the sub-basement of the Federal building, as one special agent found out. The camper shell also had numerous bruises imposed on it by low hanging tree branches that were identified much too late. But, the exterior of the camper was not as important as what it contained inside.

The interior contained communication equipment, as well as a device that could be used to see outside of the camper from one of the ceiling vents, like a submarine periscope. This was the perfect solution for a fixed surveillance position in the bank building parking lot. The only other element in this equation was to ensure that the camper could be parked in the parking lot each day and in a spot that provided an unobstructed view of the door of the building. Every morning when the camper was employed, a special agent would arrive at the parking lot around five a.m.

to secure the spot. Then, another special agent would drive the camper to the parking lot an hour before the bank building opened. Surveillance agents would already be in the back, where they would spend the day observing people coming and going to and from the bank building.

The special agent who secured the appropriate parking space for the camper would drive off just as the camper appeared. The driver of the camper would then park it, lock the doors, and be picked up by the special agent who had originally secured the parking spot. Extra keys to the camper remained with the surveillance agents inside the camper in the event the vehicle had to be moved. This whole transition of securing the spot, parking the camper and then having the driver of the camper picked up by the special agent who originally secured the spot was well choreographed and observed by special agents inside the hotel rooms.

One may ask what if the Special Agents who remained in the camper throughout the day had to use the restroom? Unfortunately for the special agents inside, the camper had no bathroom facilities, but there were plenty of empty bottles in the camper to use as needed.

The last piece of this complex surveillance equation had to do with how the surveillance agents would know who actually visited Markowitz's office after entering the building. The building had multiple floors, with many offices on each floor, including Markowitz's office on the seventh floor. Agents couldn't tell from the hotel or the camper when anyone actually went into Markowitz's office. The initial thought was to have surveillance agents follow people into the building and determine exactly what office each one visited. But this would be a cumbersome and labor-intensive solution. We imagined a scene from the *Three Stooges* as multiple surveillance agents entered the bank building behind multiple visitors, all going to different elevators to various floors.

Then there was the idea of having a surveillance agent stationed outside the elevator on the seventh floor to determine who actually entered Markowitz's office. As it turned out, Markowitz's office was located adjacent to the elevators and anyone entering his office after leaving an elevator could be readily observed from nearby. PT believed, however, and rightly so, that this would prove to be awkward. Someone would eventually ask about men hanging around the elevator. The solution was to employ a hidden camera.

Another issue involved properly identifying anyone who entered Markowitz's office. This was done by the camper surveillance agents and the hotel room surveillance agents. They would determine the owners of the cars of each person who parked in the bank parking lot, entered the bank building and then entered Markowitz's office. The vehicle license plates of those who entered Markowitz's office would be run and eventually the owner of the car would be identified. But, the communication between the surveillance agents who followed folks into the building and up to the floor where they went and to the office that they visited, would have to be accurate, including a description of those folks who actually visited Markowitz's office so that the proper vehicles and associated license plates were accurately determined.

The process required accurate communication between surveillance agents who went into the bank, including a description of the individual driving the car. That information had to be communicated to the camper surveillance agents and the hotel room surveillance agents who then would have to determine exactly what cars those people arrived in.

It was a very cumbersome operation and susceptible to potential mistakes and misidentifying people. PT and Dixon decided to install a hidden camera adjacent to Markowitz's office to view everyone coming and going. A device that recorded all of the images for use as evidence and other needs was connected to the hidden camera. Both the camper surveillance agents and the hotel room surveillance agents had a monitor that showed the images captured by the hidden camera. The hidden camera was installed by DEA and IRS-CID tech agents during nighttime hours when the building was closed and after everyone, including the custodial workers had left for the evening. The managers of the bank building were contacted and gave their permission to install the hidden camera. That completed the surveillance apparatus, including the fixed points of surveillance, the camera to provide images of suspects entering Markowitz's office, and the moving surveillance agents who followed suspects leaving the bank building after visiting Markowitz's office.

The moving surveillance served to identify the destination of individuals who visited Markowitz's office in an attempt to further identify them and gather additional information. PT also established roll back surveillance operations where anyone who visited Markowitz's office and identified as a known narcotics trafficker or an associate of known narcotics traffickers were handed off to DEA to be surveilled by separate DEA surveillance teams.

There were times when individuals were observed entering the bank building carrying a satchel, duffel bag, or just a plain brown paper bag and then entering Markowitz's office. Those individuals were then observed exiting Markowitz's office and the bank building empty handed. These events caused great excitement. These individuals became prime targets for the moving surveillance teams. Occasionally, after this type of individual left the building, another person would leave Markowitz's office in possession of the exact same satchel, duffle bag or plain brown bag. This second person also became a target of the moving surveillance agents. So, one incident would generate two moving surveillance activities: the original person who carried the item into Markowitz's office, and the other person in possession of the same item leaving the office. We soon discovered that anyone who left Markowitz's office with the package always went to the Garfield Bank

From time to time, I was assigned to be part of the moving surveillance team. I can recall specifically on one occasion when I was supporting the Markowitz surveillance operation that I followed someone from the bank building to the Hollywood Branch of Garfield Bank. The moving surveillance agents were on the lookout for anyone in possession of a bright yellow duffle bag. We were certain that this person would drive directly to the Garfield Bank. So, how did we know this?

The undercover operation took shape. Our undercover agent, WP, met with Markowitz at his office to lay the groundwork for Markowitz to launder funds for WP that Markowitz believed were the proceeds of illicit narcotics transactions. But an unexpected and troubling event occurred. The office occupied by Nathan

Markowitz was on the same floor as and adjacent to an office occupied by a man named Herb Adair. Both Markowitz and Adair even shared office staff. Adair had a prior criminal record. By total happenstance, WP had interviewed Adair when he was in the Terminal Island Federal Prison. At that time, WP introduced himself to Adair as an IRS special agent. WP knew if he ran into Adair while operating as an undercover agent in the Markowitz matter, his cover would be blown, destroying the investigation and putting WP at risk. A plan was hatched by Special Agent Dixon to have WP back out of his relationship with Markowitz and introduce another undercover agent in his place. Enter JP.

JP was a very experienced undercover operative who had worked on the East Coast where he successfully infiltrated a major organized crime operation. JP's Sicilian heritage helped him look the part, with black hair and dark features that radiated Mafia. In fact, during his East Coast assignment one of the Mafia members that met JP commented that he had the map of Italy on his face. Central casting could not have provided a better candidate to serve as an Italian Mafia member.

JP began his career as an IRS Revenue Agent, auditing tax returns. He was a CPA and a Navy veteran. After working as a Revenue Agent for a few years, he heard the siren song of what was then known as the Intelligence Division. He wanted to get into a bit more adventurous position within the IRS. So, he applied for and was accepted as a Special Agent. He eventually was placed in the IRS National Office Undercover Program where he thrived.

After learning Adair's close proximity to Markowitz, WP contacted Markowitz and advised him that things were getting too hot for him in Los Angeles, and that he needed to relocate. He convinced Markowitz to meet him in Las Vegas where they could continue to discuss the plan to launder cash. During their meeting in Las Vegas, WP introduced Markowitz to JP as his associate in the narcotics business. WP advised Markowitz that JP would deliver cash to Markowitz. Markowitz invited JP to meet with him at his office to further discuss how he could clean up dirty money.

During meetings with Markowitz at his office, Markowitz explained to JP that he would set up offshore trusts, corporate entities, and associated bank accounts. He also advised that he would establish a domestic business entity so that JP would appear to have a legitimate source of income. The money laundering circuit included delivering cash to Markowitz, which was then counted and then taken to the Garfield Bank to be deposited to a nominee account. No CTRs would be filed with the Government. The funds would then be wire transferred to the off-shore bank account of the off-shore company set up by Markowitz. Markowitz explained that the funds could then be returned in the form of non-taxable loans to a domestic entity from which JP would be paid a legitimate appearing salary. Markowitz commented to JP that the IRS would love him.

JP began to deliver cash to Markowitz. One of Markowitz's employees would then take the cash to Garfield bank to be counted, then deposited to the nominee account. Then the funds would be transferred to the off-shore account from the nominee account at Garfield Bank. JP once accompanied a Markowitz employee to Garfield Bank to see firsthand how the cash was delivered and handled at the bank. This of course was a grand slam to document exactly how Garfield Bank took in the cash, failed to file the required CTRs and then arranged for the funds to be transferred to the offshore account. Except for the first transaction, which was viewed as a test, all of the cash delivered to Markowitz by JP and run through the laundering process were in amounts far above the ten thousand dollar requirement to file CTRs. Most were in six figure amounts to add credibility to JP's supposed narcotics trafficking activities. All but a small amount of the funds presented to Markowitz by JP to be laundered were ultimately returned to the US Government by the time this case was over.

The bright yellow duffle bag referenced previously was used by JP on one occasion to deliver cash to Markowitz for laundering. The moving surveillance agents, including me spotted this duffle bag in the possession of a Markowitz employee leaving Markowitz's office after JP had dropped off cash. We followed this person directly to the Hollywood branch of Garfield Bank. Knowing where this person would transport the duffle containing JP's cash, I drove ahead, parked my vehicle near the Garfield Bank and then entered the bank to observe and document the activities of the Markowitz employee. I watched the suspect walk into the Garfield Bank carrying the bright yellow duffel bag and then proceed to the back of the bank where he entered what I later learned to be a conference room. I had to come up with a reason to remain in the bank to observe what was going on, so I approached a bank employee and inquired about opening a checking account. In short order, I was seated at a desk with that bank employee going through the motions of opening a checking account. I had a great view from my vantage point of the area where the Markowitz employee entered the conference room with the yellow duffle bag.

As part of the process to open a checking account, the bank employee asked to see my driver's license. I was one of a handful of Los Angeles District CID special agents who was issued undercover identification because of the special work I did from time to time. I was about to present my undercover driver's license to the bank employee when I noticed that the license had expired. I placed my thumb over the year of the date of expiration. At the same time, the suspect walked by the desk without the bright yellow duffle bag, heading to the exit of the bank. I made a quick excuse with the bank employee and left the bank as well. We followed the suspect back to Markowitz's office.

During the course of the surveillance and undercover activities, a couple of matters arose threatening the security of the operation. On one occasion, a private investigator approached the surveillance camper parked in the building's parking lot. The investigator knocked on the door of the surveillance camper and asked the surveillance agents who they were and what they were doing. The surveillance agents provided a plausible story that satisfied the investigator who went on his way. A review of the hidden camera video revealed that the private investigator visited Markowitz's office.

Even more troubling was an incident that revealed that our surveillance radio communications were comprised and being monitored. Unfortunately, our surveillance agents didn't always practice good communications security when transmitting their radio traffic. On one occasion, one of our surveillance agents stopped at a fast-food restaurant to grab lunch. As he left his vehicle to enter the restaurant, the manager of the restaurant approached him and asked if he was a special agent. The agent said that he was. The restaurant manager advised that he just received a call from someone named Willie who asked that the special agent parking his car in the restaurant parking lot be advised that Willie was monitoring the radio transmissions and the special agent was burned.

This event sent shock waves through the entire operation. It also prompted us to obtain radios capable of transmitting and receiving scrambled transmissions so that the radio calls could not be monitored without the proper scramble code. PT attempted to identify and arrest Willie. After the scramble radios were employed in our surveillance activities, phony radio traffic continued to be transmitted on the compromised radios in an attempt to lure Willie into a situation where he could be identified and then arrested. This never happened, but at least we kept Willie busy monitoring bogus radio traffic.

Another investigative technique employed during this investigation was the grabbing of trash from Markowitz's office. We set up a routine using the hidden camera. Each evening, a couple of special agents were assigned to go to the seventh floor and hide in a utility closet pending the arrival of a custodian who would clean Markowitz's office and remove the trash from his office. The custodian would routinely enter Markowitz's office and almost immediately place the trash from that office into a trash container attached to the custodian's cart. The custodian would then re-enter Markowitz's office to complete the cleaning routine, allowing time for the agents to leave the utility closet and gather Markowitz's trash from the custodian's container.

When the custodian arrived at Markowitz's office, after he entered the office one of the agents exited the utility closet and placed a newspaper on top of the trash that was taken from other offices and already in the trash container attached to the custodians cart. This agent would then return to the utility closet. When the custodian placed the trash from Markowitz's office in the container on his cart, it would be separated by the newspaper from the trash obtained from other offices.

The stationary surveillance agent watching the hidden camera feed directed the movements of the agent grabbing the trash. That agent would notify the agents hiding in the utility closet when the custodian arrived and initially entered Markowitz's office allowing one of the agents to hurriedly place a newspaper on top of the trash that was already in the custodian's trash container, and then return to the utility closet. When the custodian exited Markowitz's office and dumped the Markowitz trash into the container on his cart, the agent watching the camera feed would let the closeted agents know when the coast was clear and they could recover the trash removed from Markowitz's office. The agents would deposit other trash in the custodian's container so the custodian wouldn't notice that trash had been removed.

The trash taken from Markowitz's office was examined by members of Dixon's team for leads to other potential investigative targets and other potentially valuable evidence. We had a saying: "Trash talks". On one occasion, after the Willie incident, a telephone message slip was recovered from Markowitz's trash. The caller was identified as Willie. Because of this and because of the prior incident involving the surveillance camper, Dixon's team in consultation with AUSA Robert Perry decided to plan for and execute a takedown of this operation as soon as possible.

During this investigation, I was assigned to take over the management of the surveillance operation. PT received what was euphemistically termed by agents a "Battlefield commission" and promoted to group manager. Since I had a great deal of experience in surveillance operations, I was selected by Dixon to take PT's place in managing the Operation Bendix surveillance activities. This job didn't last too long as the entire operation was taken down a short time after I assumed the surveillance management job.

On January 28, 1981, search warrants were executed by Dixon's team targeting Markowitz's office and various Garfield Bank locations. The homes of several Garfield Bank employees were also searched. Markowitz was arrested and interviewed by AUSA Robert Perry and Dennis Dixon. During the interview, Markowitz was given the "Get on the train before it leaves the station" speech. We wanted Markowitz to cooperate in our investigation by identifying his narcotics trafficker clients. The sacred attorney-client privilege right could be circumvented by the crime fraud exception. Markowitz told us that he would think about the option to enter a plea and cooperate in the investigation.

Late night calls are never good. I'd received many late night calls during my IRS career. One was from my son to tell me that he'd crashed his car and he needed me to pick him up. Another was from a fellow special agent advising that an undercover agent we had employed to investigate a right-wing extremist organization had been arrested. Another was from an informant to advise me that some right-wing extremists were making plans to kill a US District Court Judge.

The call I received late at night on April 3, 1981, was even more serious. That call was from JP, the Operation Bendix undercover agent. JP advised me that Nathan Markowitz had been murdered earlier in the day. His lifeless body was found in the stairwell of a Century City parking structure. He had sustained multiple gunshot wounds, including one to his head. He had fifty-one thousand dollars in cash on him when his body was discovered, so this murder was not incidental to a robbery. It was a hit and the cash not taken sent a message regarding why he was murdered. JP said he needed to disappear and wouldn't talk or meet with anyone but me. He said that he would call me again the next day.

After the call from JP, I telephoned the Chief of the Los Angeles District, Ron Saranow. I briefed Ron as to what JP told me and Ron instructed me to find a safe location to hide JP. Ron said that he didn't care what it cost to secure JP. He said he would get funding approved to pay for the expenses. I then contacted the others involved in this matter, including Dixon and PT, and briefed them as well. I specifically advised Dixon that I was going to make arrangements for JP to be secured in a safe location.

The next day, I went about the business of attempting to locate a safe house to hide JP. I wanted to identify a fairly large apartment complex where JP could get lost in the maze of units. I found one on a major street in the San Fernando Valley. I contacted the manager of the complex, and used my undercover name and associated under cover identification to rent an apartment.

The rental application asked for the name of my employer and I used Vince Paoli Enterprises. I explained to the complex manager that Vince Paoli was my uncle and that I worked for him. Vince Paoli was the undercover name for WP, the original IRS-CID undercover agent assigned to Operation Bendix. I also told the complex manager that I was relocating to California from Oregon. I hoped that there wouldn't be much in the way of credit checks as I didn't have any backstop in Oregon. Lucky, there weren't, and I paid the security deposit and first month's rent with my undercover credit card.

I immediately contacted WP to alert him that he might get a call from an apartment complex manager to confirm my employment with my uncle Vince. WP said that he would back up my story.

I gave the "Safe house" information to JP and asked that he meet me there. He approved of my selection and was confident that he would be safe, particularly since everything was registered in my undercover name, including the utilities.

JP eventually met with the chief and Dixon. The process of preparing for prosecution of the remaining defendants began and JP felt safe enough to participate.

On July 23, 1981, a Federal Grand Jury in Los Angeles indicted Garfield Bank and seven individuals, including the bank's chairman and two former Vice Presidents for willful failure to file CTRs and conspiracy to defraud the Government. The willful failure to file CTRs pertained to twenty-nine cash transactions, ranging in amounts from $36,020 to $491.790, totaling $3.3 million over a two-year period.

Several defendants were found guilty on all counts via a jury trial. The President and CEO, as well as the bank via a bank officer pled guilty. Except for the President and CEO, who was sixty-five years old and in extremely poor health, all of the convicted defendants were sentenced to prison time.

Nathan Markowitz, was judged by a higher authority. As of the publication of this book, his killer has not been identified. During the course of the investigation to identify who killed Nathan Markowitz, a very prominent Los Angeles-based criminal defense attorney became a subject of interest. This attorney specialized in representing major narcotics traffickers. The attorney was never charged with Markowitz's murder and this is still a cold case in the files of the Los Angeles Police Department.

As a postscript to the Markowitz murder, the attorney who became a subject of interest to the investigators was once asked directly by an acquaintance if he was involved in the murder of Nathan Markowitz.

The attorney answered this question with a question; "Would you think less of me if I answered no?" An odd answer to the original question to be sure.

The online records of the California State Bar simply reflect "deceased" in its entry for Nathan Markowitz, State Bar Number 38456. To the casual observer, the word deceased means nothing more than the person is dead. To me and the others who were involved in Operation Bendix, the word deceased has a much more ominous meaning. A victim of an execution with a message; people who talk don't live very long.

www.ingramcontent.com/pod-product-compliance
Lightning Source LLC
Chambersburg PA
CBHW021454210526
45463CB00002B/774